The Vegetarian Life

200 Recipes for Eating Well Without Meat

Heather M. Beaubien

I.—UNFERMENTED BREAD.

1. COLD WATER BREAD.

1-1/4 lb. fine wholemeal flour to 3/4 pint water.

Put the meal into a basin, add the water gradually, and mix with a clean, cool hand. (Bread, pastry, etc., mixed with a spoon, especially of metal, will not be so light as that mixed with a light cool hand.) Knead lightly for 20 minutes. (A little more flour may be required while kneading, as some brands of meal do not absorb so much water as others, but do not add more than is absolutely necessary to prevent the fingers sticking.) Put the dough on to a floured board and divide into four round loaves. Prick with a fork on top.

The colder the water used, the lighter the bread, and if the mixing be done by an open window so much the better, for unfermented bread is air-raised. Distilled or clean boiled rain-water makes the lightest bread. But it should be poured backwards and forwards from one jug to another several times, in order to aerate it.

Another method of mixing is the following:—Put the water into the basin first and stir the meal quickly into it with a spatula or wooden spoon. When it gets too stiff to be stirred, add the rest of the meal. Knead for two minutes, and shape into loaves as above.

BAKING.—Bake on the bare oven shelf, floored. If possible have a few holes bored in the shelf. This is not absolutely necessary, but any tinker or ironmonger will perforate your shelf for a few pence. Better still are wire shelves, like sieves. (This does not apply to gas ovens.)

Start with a hot oven, but not too hot. To test, sprinkle a teaspoonful of flour in a patty pan, and put in the oven for five minutes. At the end of that time, if the flour is a light golden-brown colour, the oven is right. Now put in the bread and keep the heat of the oven well up for half an hour. At the end of this time turn the loaves. Now bake for another hour, but do not make up the fire again. Let the oven get slightly cooler. The same result may perhaps be obtained by moving to a cooler shelf. It all depends on the oven. But always start with a hot oven, and after the first half hour let the oven get cooler.

Always remember, that the larger the loaves the slower must be the baking, otherwise they will be overdone on the outside and underdone in the middle.

Do not open the oven door oftener than absolutely necessary.

If a gas oven is used the bread must be baked on a baking sheet placed on a sand tin. A sand tin is the ordinary square or oblong baking tin, generally supplied with gas stoves, filled with silver sand. A baking sheet is simply a piece of sheet-iron, a size smaller than the oven shelves, so that the heat may pass up and round it. Any ironmonger will cut one to size for a few pence. Do not forget to place a vessel of water (hot) in the bottom of the oven. This is always necessary in a gas oven when baking bread, cakes or pastry.

It must not be forgotten that ovens are like children they need understanding. The temperature of the kitchen and the oven's nearness to a window or door will often make a difference of five or ten minutes in the time needed for baking. One gas oven that I knew never baked well in winter unless a screen was put before it to keep away draughts!

ROLLS.—If you desire to get your bread more quickly it is only a question of making smaller loaves. Little rolls may be cut out with a large egg-cup or small pastry cutter, and these take any time from twenty minutes to half an hour.

2. EGG BREAD.

9 ozs. fine wholemeal, 1 egg, a bare 1/2 pint milk and water, butter size of walnut.

Put butter in a qr. qtn. tin (a small square-cornered tin price 6-1/2d. at most ironmongers) and let it remain in hot oven until it boils. Well whisk egg, and add to it the milk and water. Sift into this liquid the wholemeal, stirring all the time. Pour this batter into the hot buttered tin. Bake in a very hot oven for 50 minutes, then move to a cooler part for another 50 minutes. When done, turn out and stand on end to cool.

3. GEM BREAD.

Put into a basin a pint of cold water, and beat it for a few minutes in order to aerate it as much as possible. Stir gently, but quickly, into this as much fine wholemeal as will make a batter the consistency of thick cream. It should just drop off the spoon. Drop this batter into very hot greased gem pans. Bake for half an hour in a hot oven. When done, stand on end to cool. They may appear to be a little hard on first taking out of the oven, but when cool they should be soft, light and spongy. When properly made, the uninitiated generally refuse to believe that they do not contain eggs or baking-powder.

There are proper gem pans, made of cast iron (from 1s.) for baking this bread, and the best results are obtained by using them. But with a favourable oven I have got pretty good results from the ordinary baking-tins with depressions, the kind used for baking small cakes. But these are a thinner make and apt to produce a tough crust.

4. HOT WATER ROLLS.

This bread has a very sweet taste. It is made by stirring boiling water into any quantity of meal required, sufficient to form a stiff paste. Then take out of the basin on to a board and knead quickly with as much more flour as is needed to make it workable. Cut it into small rolls with a large egg-cup or small vegetable cutter. The quicker this is done the better, in order to retain the heat of the water. Bake from 20 to 30 minutes.

5. OATCAKE.

Mix medium oatmeal to a stiff paste with cold water. Add enough fine oatmeal to make a dough. Roll out very thinly. Bake in sheets, or cut into biscuits with a tumbler or biscuit cutter. Bake on the bare oven shelf, sprinkled with fine oatmeal, until a very pale brown. Flour may be used in place of the fine oatmeal, as the latter often has a bitter taste that many people object to. The cause of this bitterness is staleness, but it is not so noticeable in the coarse or medium oatmeal. Freshly ground oatmeal is quite sweet.

6. RAISIN LOAF.

1 lb. fine wholemeal, 6 oz. raisins, 2 oz. Mapleton's nutter, water.

Well wash the raisins, but do not stone them or the loaf will be heavy. If the stones are disliked, seedless raisins, or even sultanas, may be used, but the large raisins give rather better results. Rub the nutter into the flour, add the raisins, which should be well dried after washing, and mix with enough water to form a dough which almost, but not quite drops from the spoon. Put into a greased tin, which should be very hot, and bake in a hot oven at first. At the end of twenty minutes to half an hour the loaf should be slightly browned. Then move to a cooler shelf, and bake until done. Test with a knife as for ordinary cakes.

For this loaf a small, deep, square-cornered tin is required (price 6-1/2d.), the same as for the egg loaf. 3 ozs. fresh dairy butter may be used in place of the 2 ozs. nutter.

7. SHORTENED BREAD.

Into 1 lb. wholemeal flour rub 4 ozs. nutter or 5 ozs. butter. Mix to a stiff dough with cold water. Knead lightly but well. Shape into small buns about 1 inch thick. Bake for an hour in a moderate oven.

II.—SOUPS.

Soups are of three kinds—clear soups, thick soups, and purées. A clear soup is made by boiling fruit or vegetables (celery, for example) until all the nourishment is extracted, and then straining off the clear liquid. A little sago or macaroni is generally added and cooked in this. When carrots and turnips are used, a few small pieces are cut into dice or fancy shapes, cooked separately, and added to the strained soup. Thick soups always include some farinaceous ingredients for thickening (flour, pea-flour, potato, etc.). Purées are thick soups composed of any vegetable or vegetables boiled and rubbed through a sieve. This is done, a little at a time, with a wooden spoon. A little of the hot liquor is added to the vegetable from time to time to assist it through.

1. BARLEY BROTH.

1 carrot, 1 turnip, 4 leeks or 3 small onions, 4 sprigs parsley, 4 sticks celery, 1 tea-cup pearl barley, 3 qts. water. (The celery may be omitted if desired, or, when in season, 1 tea-cup green peas may be substituted.)

Scrub clean (but do not peel) the carrot and turnip. Wash celery, parsley, and barley. Shred all the vegetables finely; put in saucepan with the water. Bring to the boil and slowly simmer for 5 hours. Add the chopped parsley and serve.

2. CREAM OF BARLEY SOUP.

Make barley broth as in No. 1. Then strain it through a wire strainer. Squeeze it well, so as to get the soup as thick as possible, but do not rub the barley through. Skin 1/2 lb. tomatoes, break in halves, and cook to a pulp very gently in a closed saucepan (don't add water). Add to the barley soup, boil up once, and serve.

In cases of illness, especially where the patient is suffering from intestinal trouble, after preparing as above, strain through a fine muslin. It should also be prepared with distilled, or clean boiled rain-water.

3. CLEAR CELERY SOUP.

1 head celery, 2 tablespoons sago, 2 qts. water.

Wash the celery, chop into small pieces, and stew in the water for 2 hours. Strain. Wash the sago, add it to the clear liquid, and cook for 1 hour.

For those who prefer a thick soup, pea-flour may be added. Allow 1 level tablespoon to each pint of soup. Mix with a little cold water, and add to the boiling soup. One or two onions may also be cooked with the celery, if liked.

4. CHESTNUT SOUP.

1 lb. chestnuts, 1-1/2 oz. nutter or butter, 2 tablespoons chopped parsley, 1 tablespoon wholemeal flour, 1-1/2 pints water.

First put on the chestnuts (without shelling or pricking) in cold water, and boil for an hour. Then remove shells and put the nuts in an enamelled saucepan with the fat. Fry for 10 minutes. Add the flour gradually, stirring all the time, then add the water. Cook gently for half an hour. Lastly, add the parsley, boil up, and serve.

It is rather nicer if the flour is omitted, the necessary thickness being obtained by rubbing the soup through a sieve before adding the parsley. Those who do not object to milk may use 1 pint milk and 1 pint water in place of the 1-1/2 pints water.

5. FRUIT SOUP.

Fruit soups are used extensively abroad, although not much heard of in England. But they might be taken at breakfast with advantage by those vegetarians who have given up the use of tea, coffee and cocoa, and object to, or dislike, milk. The recipe given here is for apple soup, but pears, plums, etc., may be cooked in exactly the same way.

1 lb. apples, 1 qt. water, sugar and flavouring, 1 tablespoon sago.

Wash the apples and cut into quarters, but do not peel or core. Put into a saucepan with the water and sugar and flavouring to taste. When sweet, ripe apples can be obtained, people with natural tastes will prefer no addition of any kind. Otherwise, a little cinnamon, cloves, or the yellow part of lemon rind may be added. Stew until the apples are soft. Strain through a sieve, rubbing the apple pulp through, but leaving cores, etc., behind. Wash the sago, add to the strained soup, and boil gently for 1 hour. Stir now and then, as the sago is apt to stick to the pan.

6. HARICOT BEAN SOUP.

2 heaped breakfast-cups beans, 2 qts. water, 3 tablespoons chopped parsley or 1/2 lb. tomatoes, nut or dairy butter size of walnut, 1 tablespoon lemon juice.

For this soup use the small white or brown haricots. Soak overnight in 1 qt. of the water. In the morning add the rest of the water, and boil until soft. It may then be rubbed through a sieve, but this is not imperative. Add the chopped parsley, the lemon juice, and the butter. Boil up and serve. If tomato pulp is preferred for flavouring instead of parsley, skin the tomatoes and cook slowly to pulp (without water) before adding.

7. LENTIL SOUP.

4 breakfast-cups lentils, 1 carrot, 1 turnip, 2 onions, 4 qts. water, 4 sticks celery, 2 teaspoons herb powder, 1 tablespoon lemon juice, 1 oz. butter.

Either the red, Egyptian lentils, or the green German lentils may be used for this soup. If the latter, soak overnight. Stew the lentils very gently in the water for 2 hours, taking off any scum that rises. Well wash the vegetables, slice them, and add to the soup. Stew for 2 hours more. Then rub through a sieve, or not, as preferred. Add the lemon juice, herb powder, and butter (nut or dairy), and serve.

8. MACARONI SOUP.

1/2 lb. small macaroni, 2 qts. water or vegetable stock, 3/4 lb. onions or 1 lb. tomatoes.

Break the macaroni into small pieces and add to the stock when nearly boiling. Cook with the lid off the saucepan until the macaroni is swollen and very tender. (This will take about an hour.) If onions are used for flavouring, steam separately until tender, and add to soup just before serving. If tomatoes are used, skin and cook slowly to pulp (without water) before adding. If the vegetable stock is already strong and well-flavoured, no addition of any kind will be needed.

9. PEA SOUP.

Use split peas, soak overnight, and prepare according to recipe given for lentil soup.

10. POTATO SOUP.

Peel thinly 2 lbs. potatoes. (A floury kind should be used for this soup.) Cut into small pieces, and put into a saucepan with enough water to cover them. Add three large onions (sliced), unless tomatoes are preferred for flavouring. Bring to the boil, then simmer until the potatoes are cooked to a mash. Rub through a sieve or beat with a fork. Now add 3/4 pint water or 1 pint milk, and a little nutmeg if liked. Boil up and serve.

If the milk is omitted, the juice and pulp of two or three tomatoes may be added, and the onions may be left out also.

11. P.R. SOUP.

1 head celery, 4 large tomatoes, 4 qts. water, 4 large English onions, 3 tablespoons coarsely chopped parsley.

This soup figures often in the diet sheet of the Physical Regenerationists for gouty and rheumatic patients, but in addition to being a valuable medicine on account of its salts, it is the most delicious clear soup that I know of. To make: chop the ingredients to dice, cover closely, and simmer until the quantity of liquid is reduced to one half.

12. P.R. BEEF TEA SUBSTITUTE.

1/4 pint pearl barley, 1/4 pint red lentils, 2 qts. cold bran water, flavouring.

To make the bran water, boil 1 measure of bran with 4 measures of water for not less than 30 minutes. Simmer together the barley, lentils, and bran water for 3 hours. To flavour, put 4 ozs. butter or 3 ozs. nutter into a pan with 1 lb. sliced onions. Shake over fire until brown, but do not let them burn or the flavour of the soup will be spoilt. Add these to the stock at the end of the first hour. Any other vegetable liked may be chopped to dice and added.

Tomato may be substituted for the onion if preferred and no fat used. Strain through a hair sieve, and serve the clear liquid after boiling up.

13. SAGO SOUP.

6 ozs. sago, 2 qts. stock, juice of 1 lemon.

Wash the sago and soak it for 1 hour. Put it in a saucepan with the lemon juice and stock, and stew for 1 hour.

14. TOMATO SOUP.

1 qt. water or white stock, 1 lb. tomatoes.

Slice the tomatoes, and simmer very gently in the water until tender. Rub through a sieve. Boil up and serve.

III.—SAVOURY DISHES.

The recipes following are intended to be used as substitutes for meat, fish, etc.

The body needs for its sustenance water, mineral salts, [Footnote: I allude to mineral salts as found in the vegetable kingdom, not to the manufactured salts, like the ordinary table salt, etc., which are simply poisons when taken as food.] fats and oils, carbo-hydrates (starch and sugar), and proteids (the flesh and muscle-forming elements). All vegetable foods (in their natural state) contain all these elements, and, at a pinch, human life might be supported on any one of them. I say "at a pinch" because if the nuts, cereals and pulses were ruled out of the dietary, it would, for most people, be deficient in fat and proteid. Wholewheat, according to a physiologist whose work is one of the standard books on the subject, is a perfectly-proportioned, complete food. Hence it is possible to live entirely on good bread and water.

Nuts are the best substitute for flesh meat. Next in order come the pulses. After these come wholewheat and unpolished rice. Both nuts and pulses contain, like flesh meat, a large quantity of proteid in a concentrated form. No one needs more than 1/4 lb. per day, at most, of either. (Eggs, of course, are a good meat substitute, so far as the percentage of proteid is concerned.)

1. ALMONDS, ROASTED.

Take any quantity of shelled almonds and blanch by pouring boiling water on them. The skins can then be easily removed. Lay the blanched almonds on a tin, and bake to a pale yellow colour. On no account let them brown, as this develops irritating properties. To be eaten with vegetable stews and pies. (That is, with any stew or pie which contains neither nuts nor pulse.)

2. CHESTNUTS, BOILED.

An excellent dish for children and persons with weak digestive powers. The chestnuts need not be peeled or pricked, but merely well covered with cold water and brought to the boil, after which they should boil for a good half hour. Drain off the water and serve hot. They may also be boiled, peeled, mashed and eaten with hot milk.

3. CHESTNUT SAVOURY.

Boil for 15 minutes. Shell. Fry in a very little nut fat for 10 minutes. Barely cover with water, and stew gently until tender. When done, add some chopped parsley and thicken with chestnut flour or fine wholemeal. For those who prefer it, milk and dairy butter may be substituted for the water and nut fat.

4. CHESTNUT PIE.

1 lb. chestnuts, 1/2 lb. tomatoes, short crust.

Boil the chestnuts for half an hour. Shell. Skin the tomatoes and cut in slices. Well grease a small pie-dish, put in the chestnuts and tomatoes in alternate layers. Cover with short crust (pastry recipe No. 3) and bake until a pale brown. Serve with parsley, tomato, or white sauce.

5. CHESTNUT RISSOLES.

1 lb. chestnuts, 1 tablespoon chopped parsley, cornflour and water or 1 egg.

Boil the chestnuts for half an hour. Shell, and well mash with a fork. Add the parsley. Dissolve 1 tablespoon cornflour in 1 tablespoon water. Use as much of this as required to moisten the chestnut, and mix it to a stiff paste. Shape into firm, round, rather flat rissoles, roll in white flour, and fry in deep oil or fat to a golden brown colour. Serve with parsley or tomato sauce.

For those who take eggs, the rissoles may be moistened and bound with a beaten egg instead of the cornflour and water. They may also be rolled in egg and bread-crumbs after flouring.

6. HARICOT BEANS, BOILED.

1/2 pint beans, 1 oz. butter, water, 1 teaspoon lemon juice.

The small white or brown haricots should be used for this dish. Wash well, and soak overnight in the water. In the morning put in a saucepan in the same water and bring to the boil. Simmer slowly for 3 hours. When done they mash readily and look floury. Drain off any water not absorbed. Add the butter and lemon juice, and shake over the fire until hot. Serve with parsley or white sauce.

7. HARICOT RISSOLES.

1/2 pint haricots, 1 oz. butter, 1 medium onion, water, 1 teaspoon lemon juice, 1 teaspoon mixed herbs, or 1 tablespoon chopped parsley.

Cook the haricots as in preceding recipe. Mash well with a fork, add the onion finely grated, and the parsley or herbs. (This may be omitted if preferred.) Form into firm, round, rather flat rissoles. Roll in white flour. Fry in deep oil or fat to a golden brown colour. Serve with tomato sauce, brown gravy, or parsley sauce.

8. LENTILS, STEWED.

1 cup lentils, 1-1/2 cups water, butter (size of walnut), 1 teaspoon lemon juice.

Use either the red Egyptian, or the green German lentils. Wash well in several waters, drain, and put to soak overnight in the water. Use this same water for cooking. Cook very slowly until the lentils are soft and dry. They should just absorb the quantity of water given. (If cooked too quickly it may be necessary to add a little more.) A little thyme or herb powder may be cooked with the lentils, if liked. When done, drain off any superfluous water, add the butter and the lemon juice, shake over the fire until hot. Serve with baked potatoes and tomato sauce.

9. LENTIL PASTE.

1/2 pint red lentils, 1/2 pint bread-crumbs, 2 ozs. butter or 1-1/2 oz. nutter, 2 teaspoons lemon juice, 1/2 a nutmeg.

Well wash the lentils and place on the fire with just enough water to cover them. Simmer gently until quite soft. Add the butter, lemon juice, nutmeg, and bread-crumbs. Stir well, heat to boiling point, and cook for 10 minutes. Put in jars, and when cold pour some melted butter or nutter on the top. Tomato juice may be used in place of the lemon juice if preferred.

10. LENTIL AND LEEK PIE.

2 cups lentils, 12 small leeks, 4 cups water, short crust.

Put the lentils, water, and leeks, finely shredded, into a covered jar or basin. Bake in a slow oven until done. Put into a greased pie-dish and cover with short crust. (If lentils are very dry, add a little more water.) Bake. Serve with boiled potatoes, brown gravy, and any vegetable in season, except spinach or artichokes.

11. LENTIL RISSOLES.

1 teacup red lentils, 2 teacups bread-crumbs, or 1 teacup kornules, cornflour or egg, 1-1/2 teacups water, 4 medium-sized onions, 1 grated lemon rind, 2 teaspoons mixed herbs.

Cook the lentils slowly in a saucepan with the water until they are soft and dry. Steam the onions. If Kornules are used, add as much boiling water to them as they will only just absorb. If bread-crumbs are used, do not moisten them. Add the grated yellow part of the lemon rind and the herbs. Mix all the ingredients well together and slightly moisten with rather less than a tablespoonful of water in which is dissolved a teaspoonful of raw cornflour. This is important, as it takes the place of egg for binding purposes. Shape into round, flat rissoles, roll in white flour, and fry in boiling oil or fat until a golden-brown colour.

A beaten egg may be used for binding in place of the cornflour, and the rissoles may be dipped in egg and rolled in breadcrumbs before frying.

Serve hot with brown gravy or tomato sauce. Or cold with salad.

12. MACARONI AND TOMATO.

1/4 lb. macaroni, 1 oz. butter, 1/2 lb. tomatoes, parsley.

Use the best quality of macaroni. The smaller kinds are the most convenient as they cook more quickly. Spargetti is a favourite kind with most cooks. Break the macaroni into small pieces and drop it into fast boiling water. Cook with the lid off until quite tender. Be particular about this, as underdone macaroni is not a pleasant dish. (With a little practise the cook will be able to calculate how much water is needed for it all to be absorbed by the time the macaroni is done.) When done, drain well, add the butter, and shake over the fire until hot.

While the macaroni is cooking, skin the tomatoes, break in halves, and put into a tightly-covered saucepan. (Do not add water.) Set at the side of the stove to cook very slowly. They should never boil. When reduced to pulp they are done.

Pile the macaroni in the middle of a rather deep dish, and sprinkle with chopped parsley. Pour the tomato round and serve.

13. MUSHROOM AND TOMATO.

Many food reformers consider mushrooms to be unwholesome, and indeed, in the ordinary way, they are best left alone. But if they can be obtained quite fresh, and are not the forced, highly-manured kinds, I do not think they are injurious. But the very large variety, commonly called horse mushrooms, should not be eaten.

Peel and stalk the mushrooms. Examine them carefully for maggots. Fry in just enough nutter to prevent them sticking to the pan. Cook until quite tender. Pile on a warm, deep dish. Slice the tomatoes and fry in the same pan, taking care not to add more nutter than is absolutely necessary. When tender, arrange the tomato slices round and on the mushrooms. Pour a tablespoonful or more, according to the amount cooked, of hot water into the pan. Stir well and boil up. Pour the gravy formed over the mushrooms, and serve.

14. NUT COOKERY.

For nut-cookery, a nut mill or food chopper of some kind is necessary. A tiny food chopper, which can be regulated to chop finely or coarsely as required, may be bought for 3s. at most food-reform stores. It also has an attachment which macerates the nuts so as to produce "nut butter." The larger size at 5s. is the more convenient for ordinary use. If only one machine can be afforded, the food chopper should be the one chosen, as it can also be used for vegetables, breadcrumbs, etc. The nut-mill proper flakes the nuts, it will not macerate them, and is useful for nuts only. But flaked nuts are a welcome and pretty addition to fruit salads, stewed fruits, etc.

If the nuts to be milled or ground clog the machine, put them in a warm oven until they just begin to change colour. Then let them cool, and they will be found crisp and easy to work. But avoid doing this if possible, as it dries up the valuable nut oil.

15. NUT ROAST.

2 breakfast cups bread-crumbs, 2 medium Spanish onions, or 2 tomatoes, 2 breakfast cups ground nuts, nutter.

Any shelled nuts may be used for this roast. Some prefer one kind only; others like them mixed. Almonds, pine-kernels, new Brazil nuts, and new walnuts are nice alone. Old hazel nuts and walnuts are nicer mixed with pine-kernels. A good mixture is one consisting of equal quantities of blanched almonds, walnuts, hazel nuts, and pine-kernels; where strict economy is a consideration, peanuts may be used. Put a few of each kind alternately into the food chopper and grind until you have enough to fill two cups. Mix with the same quantity breadcrumbs. Grate the onions, discard all tough pieces, using the soft pulp and juice only with which to mix the nuts and crumbs to a very stiff paste. If onions are disliked, skin and mash two tomatoes for the same purpose. Or one onion and one tomato may be used.

Well grease a pie-dish, fill it with the mixture, spread a few pieces of nutter (or butter) on the top, and bake until brown.

Another method.—For those who use eggs, the mixing may be done with a well-beaten egg. The mixture may also be formed into an oblong roast, greased, and baked on a tin. Serve with brown gravy or tomato sauce.

16. NUT RISSOLES.

Make a stiff mixture as for nut roast, add a tablespoonful savoury herbs if liked. Form into small, flat rissoles, roll them in white flour, and fry in deep fat or oil. Serve hot with gravy, or cold with salad.

17. NUT PASTE.

A nourishing paste for sandwiches is made by macerating pine-kernels with the "nut butter" attachment of the food chopper, and flavouring with a little fresh tomato juice. This must be used the same day as made as it will not keep.

Another method.—Put equal quantities of pea-nuts and pine-kernels into a warm oven until the latter just begin to colour. The skins of the pea-nuts will now be found to rub easily off. Put the mixed nuts through the macerator and mix to a stiff paste with some tomato juice. Put in a saucepan and heat to boiling point. Pour melted butter over top. This may be kept until the next day, but no longer.

18. NUT AND LENTIL ROAST AND RISSOLES.

Proceed as for nut roast or rissoles, but use cold stewed lentils (see recipe) in the place of bread-crumbs.

19. PINE KERNELS, ROASTED.

Put on a tin in a warm oven, bake until a very pale golden colour. On no account brown. Serve with vegetable stew.

20. RICE, BOILED.

1 cup unpolished rice, 3 cups water.

Put the rice on in cold water, and bring it gradually to the boil. Boil hard for 5 minutes, stirring once or twice. Draw it to the side of the stove, where it is comparatively cool, or, if a gas stove is used, put the saucepan on an asbestos mat and turn the gas as low as possible. The water should now gradually steam away, leaving the rice dry and well cooked. Serve plain or with curry.

21. RICE, SAVOURY.

Cook rice as in foregoing recipe. Fry a small, finely-chopped onion in very little fat. Add this to the cooked rice with butter the size of a walnut, and a pinch of savoury herbs. Shake over the fire until hot. Serve with peeled baked potatoes and baked tomatoes.

22. RICE AND EGG FRITTERS.

Mix any quantity of cold boiled rice with some chopped parsley and well-beaten egg. Beat the mixture well, form into small fritters, roll in egg and bread-crumbs or white flour, and fry to a golden brown. Serve with egg sauce.

23. TOAD-IN-THE-HOLE.

Grease a pie-dish. Put in it 2 or 3 small firm tomatoes, or some small peeled mushrooms. Make a batter as for Yorkshire pudding and pour over. Bake until golden brown.

24. VEGETABLE MARROW, STUFFED.

1 medium marrow, 2 ozs. butter or 1-1/2 oz. nutter, 1 dessertspoon sage, 2 medium onions, 4 tablespoons bread-crumbs, 1 tablespoon milk or water.

Chop the onion small and mix with the bread-crumbs, sage, and milk or water. Peel the marrow and scoop out the pith and pips. (Cut it in halves to do this, or, better still, if possible cut off one end and scoop out inside with a long knife.) Tie the two halves together with clean string. Stuff the marrow and bake for 40 minutes on a well-greased tin. Lay some of the nutter on top and baste frequently until done. It should brown well. Serve with brown gravy or white sauce.

25. VEGETABLE MARROW AND NUT ROAST.

Make a paste as for nut roast (see recipe). Peel marrow, scoop out the inside, and stuff. Bake from 40 minutes to an hour in a hot oven. Baste frequently.

26. VEGETARIAN IRISH STEW.

1 lb. tomatoes, 7 small Spanish onions, 8 medium potatoes, 1 oz. nutter or butter, 2 small carrots or parsnips, or 1 cup fresh green peas.

A saucepan with a close-fitting lid, and, if a gas stove is used, an asbestos mat (price 3-1/2d. at any ironmongers) is needed for this stew. Skin the tomatoes, peel and quarter the onions, and put them into the saucepan with the nutter and shut down the lid tightly. If a gas or oil flame is used, turn it as low as possible. Put the asbestos mat over this and stand the saucepan upon it. At the end of 1 hour the onions should be gently stewing in a sea of juice. Add the potatoes now (peeled and cut in halves). Also the peas, if in season. Cook for another hour. If carrot or parsnip is the extra vegetable used, cut into quarters and put in with the onions. When done, the onions are quite soft, and the potatoes, etc., just as if they had been cooked in a steamer.

Note that the onions and tomatoes must be actually stewing when the potatoes are put in, as the latter cook in the steam arising from the former.

Consequently, they should be laid on top of the onions, etc., not mixed with them. If cooked on the kitchen range, a little longer time may be needed, according to the state of the fire. Never try to cook quickly, or the juice will dry up and burn. The slow heat is the most important point.

27. VEGETABLE PIE.

Cook the vegetables according to recipe for vegetable stew. When cold put in a pie-dish (gravy and all) and cover with short crust. Bake for half an hour. If preferred, the vegetables may be covered with cold mashed potatoes in place of pie-crust. Top with a few small pieces of nutter, and bake until brown.

28. VEGETABLE STEW.

1 carrot, 1 turnip, 1 potato, 1 parsnip, 2 Jerusalem artichokes, 2 onions, 2 tomatoes, 1 teaspoon lemon juice, nutter size of small walnut.

Scrub and scrape the carrot, turnip, parsnip and artichokes. Peel the potato and onions. Shred the onions and put them into a stew-pan with the nutter. Shake over the fire, and fry until brown, but do not burn or the flavour of the stew will be completely spoilt. Cut the carrot and parsnip and potato into quarters, the artichokes into halves, and put into the stew-pan with the onions. Barely cover with water. Bring to the boil and stew very gently until tender. Skin the tomatoes, break in halves, and cook slowly to a pulp in a separate pan. Add these, with the lemon juice, to the stew, and slightly thicken with a little wholemeal flour just before serving.

IV.—CASSEROLE COOKERY.

Casserole is the French word for stew-pan. But "Casserole Cookery" is a phrase used to denote cookery in earthenware pots. It commends itself especially to food-reformers, as the slow cookery renders the food more digestible, and the earthenware pots are easier to keep clean than the ordinary saucepan. The food is served up in the pot in which it is cooked, this being simply placed on a dish. A large pudding-basin covered with a plate may be used in default of anything better. A clean white serviette is generally pinned round this before it comes to table. Various attractive-looking brown crocks are sold for the purpose. But anyone who possesses the old-fashioned "beef-tea" jar needs nothing else. It is important to ensure that a new casserole does not crack the first time of using. To do this put the casserole into a large, clean saucepan, or pail, full of clean cold water. Put over a fire or gas ring, and bring slowly to the boil. Boil for 10 minutes and then stand aside to cool. Do not take the casserole out until the water is cold.

1. FRENCH SOUP.

2 carrots, 1 turnip, 1 leek, 1 stick celery, 1/2 cabbage, 1 bay leaf, 2 cloves, 6 peppercorns, 3 qts. water.

Scrape and cut up carrots and turnip. Slice the leek, and cut celery into dice. Shred the cabbage. Put into the jar with the water, and place in a moderate oven, or on the top of a closed range. If it is necessary to use a gas ring, turn very low and stand jar on an asbestos mat. Bring to the boil slowly and then simmer for 2-1/2 hours.

2. HOT POT.

1 lb. potatoes, 2 carrots, 1 large onion, 1 turnip, 1/4 lb. mushrooms or 1/2 lb. tomatoes, 1 pint stock or water.

Wash, peel, and slice thickly the potatoes. Wash and scrape and slice the carrots and turnip. Skin the tomatoes or mushrooms. Put in the jar in alternate layers. Moisten with the stock or water. Cook as directed in recipe 1 for 1-1/2 hours after it first begins to simmer.

3. STEWED APPLES.

Take hard, red apples. Wash, but do not peel or core. Put in jar with cold water to reach half way up the apples. Cover closely and put in moderate oven for 2 hours after it begins to simmer. At end of 1 hour, add sugar to taste.

V.—CURRIES.

I do not recommend the use of curries. Many food-reformers eschew them altogether. But they are sometimes useful for the entertainment of meat-eating friends, or to tide over the attack of meat-craving which sometimes besets the vegetarian beginner. Of course there are curries and curries. Cheap curry powders are very much hotter than those of a better quality. When buying curry powder it is best to go to a high-class grocer and get the smallest possible tin of the best he keeps. It will last for years. Those who prefer to make their own curry powder may try Dr. Kitchener's recipe as follows:—

1. CURRY POWDER.

3 ozs. coriander seed, 2-1/2 ozs. tumeric, 1 oz. black pepper, 1/2 oz. lesser cardamoms, 1/4 oz. cinnamon, 1/4 oz. cumin seed.

Put the ingredients into a cool oven and let them remain there all night. Next day pound them thoroughly in a marble mortar, and rub through a sieve. Put the powder into a well-corked bottle.

A spice machine may be used instead of the mortar, but in that case the tumeric should be obtained ready powdered, as it is so hard that it is apt to break the machine. The various ingredients are generally only to be obtained from a large wholesale druggist.

2. EGG CURRY.

1 large onion, 1 dessertspoon curry powder, 1 oz. butter or nutter, 3 hard-boiled eggs, 1 dessertspoon tomato pulp, 1 teacup water.

Shred the onion, put it in the stew-pan with the butter, sprinkle the curry powder over, and fry gently until quite brown. Shell the eggs and cut them in halves. Add the eggs, the tomato pulp, and the water. Stir well, and simmer until the liquid is reduced to one-half. This will take about 15 minutes. Serve with plain boiled unpolished rice.

3. GERMAN LENTIL CURRY.

Use the ingredients given, and proceed exactly the same as for egg curry. But in place of eggs, take 1 breakfastcup of cold cooked German lentils (see recipe for cooking lentils). Use also 2 teacups water in place of the 1, and only 3/4 oz. butter or nutter.

4. VEGETABLE CURRY.

Use the ingredients given and proceed the same as for German lentil curry, using any cold steamed vegetables in season. The best curry, according to an Indian authority, is one made of potatoes, artichokes, carrots, pumpkin and tomatoes.

Note.—A writer in Cassell's Dictionary of Cookery says:—"A spoonful of cocoanut kernel dried and powdered gives a delicious flavour to a curry,

VII.—GRAVIES AND SAUCES.

1. BROWN GRAVY.

Fry a chopped onion in a very little nutter until a dark brown. (Do not burn, or the flavour of the gravy will be spoilt.) Drain off the fat and add 1/2 pint water. Boil until the water is brown. Strain. Return to saucepan and add flavouring to taste. A teaspoon of lemon juice and a tomato, skinned and cooked to pulp, are good additions. Or any vegetable stock may be used instead of the water.

THICK.—If thick gravy be desired, mix a dessertspoonful wholemeal flour with a little cold water. Add the boiling stock to this. Return to saucepan and boil for 3 minutes. Add a small piece of butter just before serving.

Another method.—Add a little "browning" (see recipe) to any vegetable stock. Thicken.

2. EGG SAUCE.

Make a white sauce (see recipe). Boil an egg for 20 minutes, shell, chop finely, and add to the sauce.

3. PARSLEY SAUCE.

Make a white sauce (see recipe). But if the use of milk be objected to, make the sauce of water and wholemeal flour. Allow 1 tablespoon finely-chopped parsley to each 1/2 pint of sauce. Add to the sauce, and boil up. Add a small piece of butter or nut-butter just before serving.

4. SWEET LEMON SAUCE.

2 ozs. lump sugar, 1 large lemon.

Rub the lemon rind well with the sugar. Put the sugar into a saucepan with as much water as it will just absorb. Boil to a clear syrup. Add the lemon juice. Make hot, but do not boil.

5. TOMATO SAUCE.

Pour boiling water on the tomatoes, allow to stand for 1 minute, after which the skins may be easily removed. Break the tomatoes (do not cut) and put into a closely-covered saucepan. Put on one side of the range, or an asbestos mat over a very low gas ring, and allow to cook slowly to pulp. Serve.

This simple recipe makes the most delicious sauce for those who appreciate the undiluted flavour of the tomato. But a good sauce may be made by allowing 1 teacup water or carrot stock to each teacup of pulp, boiling up and thickening with wholemeal flour. A little butter may be added just before serving.

6. WHITE SAUCE.

Allow 1 level dessertspoon cornflour to 1/2 pint milk. Mix the cornflour with a very little cold water in a basin. Pour the boiling milk into this, stirring all the time. Return to saucepan and boil 5 minutes. Add a small piece of butter just before serving.

7. BROWNING, FOR GRAVIES AND SAUCES.

Put 2 ozs. lump sugar in saucepan with as much water as it will just absorb. Boil to a clear syrup, and then simmer very gently, stirring all the time, until it is a very dark brown, almost black. It must not burn or the flavour will be spoilt. Then add a pint of water, boil for a few minutes. Put into a tightly-corked bottle and use as required.

VIII.—EGG COOKERY.

Many vegetarians discard the use of eggs and milk for principle's sake, but the majority still find them necessary as a half-way house. But no eggs at all are infinitely to be preferred to any but real new-laid eggs. The commercial "cooking-egg" is an unwholesome abomination.

1. BOILED EGGS FOR INVALIDS.

Put the egg on in cold water. As soon as it boils take the saucepan off the fire and stand on one side for 5 minutes. At the end of this time the egg will be found to be very lightly, but thoroughly, cooked.

2. BUTTERED EGGS.

3 eggs, 1 tablespoon milk, 1/2 oz. fresh butter.

Beat up the eggs and add the milk. Melt the butter in a small stew-pan. When hot, pour in the eggs and stir until they begin to set. Have ready some buttered toast. Pile on eggs and serve.

3. EGG ON TOMATO.

1 egg, 2 medium tomatoes, butter.

Skin the tomatoes. Break into halves and put them, with a very small piece of butter, into a small stew-pan. Close tightly, and cook slowly until reduced to a pulp. Break the egg into a cup and slide gently on to the tomato. Put on the stew-pan lid. The egg will poach in the steam arising from the tomato.

4. DEVILLED EGGS.

Boil eggs for 20 minutes. Remove shells. Cut in halves and take out the yolks. Well mash yolks with a very little fresh butter, melted, and curry powder to taste. Stuff the whites with the mixture, join halves together, and arrange in a dish of watercress.

5. SCRAMBLED EGG AND TOMATO.

Skin the tomatoes and cook to pulp as in the preceding recipe. Beat the egg and stir it in to the hot tomato. Cook until just beginning to set.

6. OMELET, PLAIN.

Whisk the egg or eggs lightly to a froth. Put enough butter in the frying-pan to just cover when melted. When this is hot, pour the eggs into it, and stir gently with a wooden spoon until it begins to set. Fold over and serve.

7. SAVOURY OMELET.

2 eggs, 2 tablespoons milk, 1/2 teaspoon finely-chopped parsley or mixed herbs, 1/2 a very small onion (finely minced), 1 teaspoon fresh butter.

Put butter in the omelet pan. Beat the eggs to a fine froth, stir in the milk and parsley, and pour into the hot pan. Stir quickly to prevent sticking. As soon as it sets, fold over and serve.

8. SWEET OMELET.

Proceed as in recipe for Savoury Omelet, but substitute a dessertspoon castor sugar for the onion and parsley. When set, put warm jam in the middle. Fold over and serve.

9. SOUFFLÉ OMELET.

2 eggs, 1 dessertspoon castor sugar, grated yellow part of rind of 1/2 lemon, butter.

Separate the yolks from the whites of the eggs. Beat the yolks and add sugar and lemon. Whisk the whites to a stiff froth. Mix very gently with the yolks. Pour into hot buttered pan. Fold over and serve when set. Put jam in middle or not, as preferred.

IX.—PASTRY, SWEET PUDDINGS, &c.

1. PASTRY.

Pastry should usually be made with a very fine wholemeal flour, such as the "Nu-Era." There are times, however, when concessions to guests, etc., demand the use of white flour. In such an event, use a good brand of household flour. The more refined the kind, the less nutriment it contains. Never add baking-powders of any kind.

The secret of making good pastry lies in lightly mixing with a cool hand. If a spoon must be used, let it be a wooden one. Roll in one direction only, away from the person. If you must give a backward roll, let it be only once. Above all, roll lightly and little. The quicker the pastry is made the better.

2. PUFF PASTE.

1/2 lb. fresh-butter or 6 ozs. Mapleton's nutter, 1 yolk of egg or 1 teaspoon lemon juice, 1/2 lb. flour.

If butter is used, wrap it in a clean cloth and squeeze well to get rid of water. Beat the yolk of egg slightly. Put the flour on the paste board in a heap. Make a hole in the centre and put in the yolk of egg or lemon juice, and about 1 tablespoon of water. The amount of water will vary slightly according to the kind of flour, and less will be required if egg is used instead of lemon juice, but add enough to make a rather stiff paste. Mix lightly with the fingers and knead until the paste is nice and workable. But do it quickly!

Next, roll out the paste to about 1/4 inch thickness. Put all the butter or nutter in the centre of this paste and wrap it up neatly therein. Stand in a cool place for 15 minutes. Next, roll it out once, and fold it over, roll it out again and fold it over. Do this lightly. Put it away again for 15 minutes. Repeat this seven times! (I do not think many food-reformers will have the time or inclination to repeat the above performance often. Speaking for myself, I have only done it once. But as no instructions about pastry are supposed to be complete without a recipe for puff-paste, I include it.) It is now ready for use.

Do not forget to keep the board and pin well floured, or the pastry will stick. If wholemeal flour is used, it is well to have white flour for the board and pin. See also that the nutter is the same consistency as ordinary butter when kept in a medium temperature. If too hard, it must be cut up and slightly warmed. If oily, it must be cooled by standing tin in very cold water.

3. SHORT CRUST.

1/2 lb. flour, 3 ozs. nutter or butter.

Rub the nutter or butter lightly into the flour. Add enough cold water to make a fairly stiff paste. Roll it out to a 1/4 inch thickness. It is now ready for use.

4. APPLE CHARLOTTE.

Apples, castor sugar, grated lemon rind, butter or nutter, bread-crumbs or Granose flakes.

Bread-crumbs make the more substantial, granose flakes the more dainty, charlotte. Use juicy apples. "Mealy" apples make a bad charlotte. If they must be used, a tablespoon or more, according to size, of water must be poured over the charlotte. Peel, core, and slice apples. Grease a pie-dish. Put in a thin layer of crumbs. On this dot a few small pieces nutter. Over this put a generous layer of chopped apple. Sprinkle with sugar and grated lemon rind. Repeat the process until the dish is full. Top with crumbs. Bake from 20 minutes to half an hour. When done, turn out on to dish, being careful not to break. Sprinkle a little castor sugar over. Serve hot or cold. Boiled custard may be served with it.

5. APPLE DUMPLINGS.

Peel and core some good cooking apples, but keep them whole. If you have no apple-corer, take out as much of the core as possible with a pointed knife-blade. Fill the hole with sugar and a clove. Make short paste and cut into squares. Fold neatly round and over apple. Bake from 30 to 45 minutes. If preferred boiled, tie each dumpling loosely in a cloth, put into boiling water and cook from 45 minutes to 1 hour.

6. APPLE AND TAPIOCA.

1/4 pint tapioca, 1 lb. apples, 1 pint water, sugar, lemon peel.

Soak the tapioca in the water overnight. Peel and core the apples, cut into quarters, stew, and put in a pie-dish. Sprinkle with sugar to taste, and the grated yellow part of a fresh lemon rind. Mix in the soaked tapioca and water. Bake about 1 hour. Serve cold, with or without boiled custard.

7. BATTER PUDDING.

2 eggs, 1 teacup flour, milk.

Well whisk the eggs. Sprinkle in the flour a spoonful at a time. Stir gently. When the batter becomes too thick to stir, thin it with a little milk. Then add more flour until it is again too thick, and again thin with the milk. Proceed in this way until all the flour is added, and then add sufficient milk to bring the batter to the consistency of rather thick cream. Have ready a very hot greased tin, pour in and bake in a hot oven until golden brown. By mixing in the way indicated above, a batter perfectly free from lumps is easily obtained.

8. BOMBAY PUDDING.

Cook a heaped tablespoon of semolina in 1/2 pint of milk to a stiff paste. Spread it on a plate to cool. (Smooth it neatly with a knife). When quite cold, cut it into four. Dip in a beaten egg and fry brown. Serve hot with lemon sauce. This may also be served as a savoury dish with parsley sauce. The quantity given above is sufficient for two people.

9. BREAD AND FRUIT PUDDING.

Line a pudding-basin with slices of bread from which the crust has been removed. Take care to fit the slices together as closely and neatly as possible. Stew any juicy fruit in season with sugar to taste. Do not add water. (Blackcurrants or raspberries and redcurrants are best for this dish.) When done, fill up the basin with the boiling fruit. Top with slices of bread fitted well in. Leave until cold. Turn out and serve.

10. BLANC MANGE, AGAR-AGAR.

1/4 oz. prepared agar-agar, 1-1/2 pints milk, sugar, flavouring.

Soak a vanilla pod, cinnamon stick, or strip of fresh lemon rind in the cold milk until flavoured to taste. Add sugar to taste. Put in a saucepan with the agar-agar, and simmer until dissolved (about 30 minutes). Pour through a hot strainer into wet mould. Turn out when cold.

11. CHOCOLATE JELLY.

1/4 oz. prepared agar-agar, 2 sticks chocolate, 1-1/2 pints milk, 1 tablespoon sugar, vanilla flavouring.

Soak a vanilla pod in the cold milk for 2 hours. Soak the agar-agar in cold water for half an hour. Squeeze water out and pull to pieces. Put it into saucepan with 1 gill milk and 1/2 gill water. Stand on one side of stove and let simmer very gently until quite dissolved. Meanwhile, dissolve chocolate in rest of milk, adding the sugar. Pour the agar-agar into the boiling chocolate through a hot strainer. This is necessary as there is generally a little tough scum on the liquid. (If put through a cold strainer, the agar-agar will set as it goes through.) When jelly is quite cold, turn out and serve.

12. CORNFLOUR SHAPE.

Stew some juicy plums or apples slowly to a pulp with sugar to taste. If apples are used, add cloves or a little grated lemon rind for flavouring. To every pint of fruit pulp allow a level tablespoon of cornflour. Dissolve the cornflour in a little cold water and stir into the boiling apple. Boil for 5 minutes, stirring all the time. Pour into a wet mould. Turn out and serve when cold.

13. CUSTARD, BOILED.

1 pint milk, 2 eggs, 1 tablespoon castor sugar, flavouring.

Put some thin strips of the yellow part of a lemon rind, or a vanilla pod, in the cold milk. Allow to stand 1 hour or more. Then take out the peel, add the sugar, and put over the fire in a double saucepan, if possible. Bring to the boil. Beat the eggs. Take the milk off the fire, let it stop boiling, and pour it slowly into the eggs, beating all the time. Put back into the saucepan over a slow fire and stir until the mixture thickens (about 20 minutes).

14. CUSTARD, HOGAN.

1 qt. milk, 8 eggs, 12 lumps sugar, 1 large tablespoon cornflour.

Flavour milk as in Boiled Custard. Put nearly all the milk and all the sugar into a 3-pint jug and stand in a saucepan of boiling water. While this is heating beat the eggs in one basin, and mix the cornflour with the remainder of the milk in another. Add the eggs to hot milk, stirring all the time, and finally add the cornflour. Stir until the mixture thickens (about 20 minutes).

15. DATE PUDDING.

This recipe is inserted especially for those who object to the use of manufactured sugar.

1/2 lb. "Ixion" plain wholemeal biscuits, 1/2 lb. dates, 2 ozs. nutter, 1 heaped tablespoon wholemeal flour, grated rind of 2 lemons, water.

Grind the biscuits to flour in the food-chopper. Wash, stone, and chop the dates. Grate off the yellow part of the lemon rinds. Rub the nutter into the biscuit-powder. Add dates, lemon peel, and flour. Mix with enough water to make a paste stiff enough for the spoon to just stand up in alone. Be very particular about this, as the tendency is to add rather too little than too much water, owing to the biscuit-powder absorbing it more slowly. Put into a greased pudding-basin or mould. Steam or boil for 5 hours. "Ixion Kornules" may be used instead of the biscuits, if preferred. They save the labour of grinding, but they need soaking for an hour in cold water before using. Well squeeze, add the other ingredients, and moisten with the water squeezed from the kornules.

Another method.—Use the recipe for Plum Pudding, leaving out all the dried fruit, almonds and sugar, substituting in their place 1 lb. dates or figs.

16. FIG PUDDING.

Use the recipe for Date Pudding, substituting for the dates washed chopped figs.

17. JAM ROLL, BOILED.

Make a short crust, roll out, spread with home-made jam, roll up, carefully fastening ends, and tie loosely in a floured pudding-cloth. Put into fast-boiling water and boil for 1 hour.

18. JAM ROLL, BAKED.

Mix the paste for the crust just a little stiffer than for the boiled pudding. Spread with jam and roll up. Bake on a greased tin for half-an-hour.

19. MILK PUDDINGS.

Nearly every housewife makes milk puddings, but only one in a hundred can make them properly. When cooked, the grains should be quite soft and encased with a rich thick cream. Failure to produce this result simply indicates that the pudding has been cooked too quickly, or that the proportion of grain to milk is too large.

Allow 2 level tablespoons, not a grain more, of cereal (rice, sago, semolina, tapioca) and 1 level tablespoon sugar to every pint of milk. Put in a pie-dish with a vanilla pod or some strips of lemon rind, and stand for an hour in a warm place, on the hob for example. Then take out the pod or peel and put into a fairly hot oven. As soon as the pudding boils, stir it well, and move to a cooler part of the oven. It should now cook very slowly for 2 hours.

20. JELLY, ORANGE.

7 juicy oranges, 1 lemon, 6 ozs. lump sugar, water, 1/4 oz. prepared agar-agar.

Rub the skins of the oranges and lemons well with some of the lumps of sugar, and squeeze the juice from the oranges and lemon. Soak the agar-agar in cold water for half an hour and then thoroughly squeeze. Warm in 1 gill of water until dissolved. Put the fruit juice, agar-agar, and enough water to make the liquid up to 1-1/2 pints, into a saucepan. Bring to the boil.

Pour through a hot strainer into a wet mould. Turn out when cold. If difficult to turn out, stand the mould in a basin of warm water for 2 or 3 seconds.

21. JELLY, RASPBERRY & CURRANT.

1 lb. raspberries, 1/2 lb. currants, 6 ozs. sugar, 1/4 oz. prepared agar-agar, 3/4 pint water.

Soak agar-agar as for Orange Jelly. Cook fruit with 1/2 pint water until well done. Strain through muslin. Warm the agar-agar until dissolved in 1 gill of water. Put the fruit juice, sugar, and agar-agar into a saucepan. If liquid measures less than 1-1/2 pints, add enough water to make up quantity. Bring to the boil, pour through a hot strainer into wet mould. Turn out when cold and serve.

22. MINCEMEAT.

1/2 lb. raisins, 1/2 lb. sultanas, 1/2 lb. currants, 1/2 lb. castor sugar, 1/4 lb. nutter, 1/2 a nutmeg, grated rind of 2 lemons, 1-1/2 lb. apples.

Well wash all the dried fruit in warm water, and allow to dry thoroughly before using. Stone the raisins, pick the sultanas, and rub the currants in a cloth to remove stalks. Wash and core the apples, but do not peel them. Put all the fruit and apple through a fine food-chopper. Add the sugar, grated lemon rind, and nutmeg. Lastly, melt the nutter and add. Stir the mixture well, put it into clean jars, and tie down with parchment covers until needed for mince pies.

23. NUT PASTRY.

Flake brazil nuts or pine-kernels in a nut mill, or chop very finely by hand. Do not put them through the food-chopper, as this pulps them together, and the pudding will be heavy. Allow 1 heaped cup of flaked nuts to 2 level cups of flour. Mix to a paste with cold water. Roll out very lightly. Cover with chopped apple and sugar, or apples and sultanas, or jam. Roll up. Tie loosely in a floured pudding-cloth. Put into fast-boiling water and boil for 1 hour.

24. PLAIN PUDDING.

1 lb. flour, 3 ozs. nutter, a full 1/2 pint water.

Rub the nutter very lightly into the flour, or chop like suet and mix in. Add the water gradually, and mix well. Put into a pudding-basin, and boil or steam for 3 hours. Turn out and serve with golden syrup, lemon sauce or jam.

25. PLUM PUDDING, CHRISTMAS.

1/2 lb. raisins, 1/2 lb. sultanas, 1/2 lb. currants, 1/2 lb. cane sugar, 1/2 lb. flour, 1/4 lb. sweet almonds, 1/4 lb. grated carrot, 1/4 lb. grated apple, 1/4 lb. nutter, grated rind of 2 lemons, 1/2 a nutmeg.

Well wash the raisins, sultanas and currants in hot water. Don't imagine that this will deprive them of their goodness. The latter is all inside the skin. What comes off from the outside is dirt, and a mixture of syrup and water through which they have been passed to improve their appearance. Rub the currants in a cloth to get off the stalks, pick the stalks from the sultanas, and stone the raisins. Put the currants and sultanas in a basin, just barely cover them with water, cover them with a plate, and put into a warm oven—until they have fully swollen, when the water should be all absorbed. (Currants treated in this way will not disagree with the most delicate child. They are abominations if not so treated.) Rub the nutter into the flour, or chop it as you would suet. Blanch the almonds by steeping them in boiling water for a few minutes: the skins may then be easily removed; chop very finely, or put through a mincer. Wash, core, and mince (but do not peel) the apples. Grate off the yellow part of the lemon rind. Mince or grate the carrots.

Mix together the flour, nutter, sugar, lemon rind, almonds and nutmeg. Then add the raisins, sultanas and currants. Lastly, add the grated carrot and apple, taking care not to lose any of the juice. Don't add any other moisture. If the directions have been exactly followed, it will be moist enough. Put it into pudding-basins or tin moulds greased with nutter, and boil or steam for 8 hours.

26. RAILWAY PUDDING.

2 eggs, 1 oz. butter, 3 ozs. flour, 2 ozs. castor sugar, 2 tablespoons milk.

Beat the butter and sugar to a cream. Separate the whites and yolks of the eggs. Beat the yolks, and add to sugar and butter. Add the flour, and lastly, stir in the whites, whisked to a froth, very gently. Have ready a hot, greased tin, pour in the mixture quickly, and bake in a very hot oven from 6 to 8 minutes. Warm some jam in a small saucepan. Slip the pudding out of the tin on to a paper sprinkled with castor sugar. Spread with jam quickly and roll up. Serve hot or cold.

27. SAGO SHAPE.

5 ozs. small sago, sugar to taste, 1-1/2 pints water, or water and fruit juice.

Wash the sago. Soak it for 4 hours. Strain off the water. Add to the strainings enough water or the juice from stewed fruit to make 1-1/2 pints liquid. Sweeten if necessary, but if the juice from stewed fruit is used it will probably be sweet enough. This dish is spoiled if made too sweet. Put the sago and 1-1/2 pints liquid into a saucepan and stew for 20 minutes. Now add the stewed fruit which you deprived of its juice, stir well, pour into a wet mould, and serve cold. Made with water only, and flavoured with a very little sugar and lemon peel, it may be served with stewed fruit.

28. SUMMER PUDDING.

Put a layer of sponge cake at the bottom of a glass dish. Cut up a tinned pine-apple (get the pine-apple chunks if possible) and fill dish, first pouring a little of the juice over the cake. Melt a very little agar-agar in the rest of the juice. (Allow half the 1/4 oz. to a pint of juice.) Pour over the mixture. Serve when cold.

29. TREACLE PUDDING.

Line a pudding-basin with short crust. Mix together in another basin some good cane golden syrup, enough bread-crumbs to thicken it, and some grated lemon rind. Put a layer of this mixture at the bottom of the pudding-basin, cover with a layer of pastry, follow with a layer of the mixture, and so on, until the basin is full. Top with a layer of pastry, tie on a floured pudding-cloth, and boil or steam for 3 hours.

30. TRIFLE, SIMPLE.

Put a layer of sponge cake at the bottom of a glass dish. Better still, use sections of good home-made jam sandwich. Pour hot boiled custard on to this until the cake is barely covered. Blanch some sweet almonds, and cut into strips. Stick these into the top of the cake until it somewhat resembles the back of a hedgehog! Serve when cold.

X.—CAKES AND BISCUITS.

Cakes need a hot oven for the first half-hour.

If possible, they should not be moved from one shelf to another, but the oven should be cooled gradually by opening the ventilators or lowering the gas. A moderate oven is needed to finish the cooking.

All fruit cakes (unless weighing less than 1 lb.) need to be baked from 1-1/2 to 2 hours. The larger the cake the slower should be the baking.

The cake tins should be lined with greased paper.

If a gas oven is used, stand the cake tin on a sand tin (see Cold Water Bread).

If the cake becomes sufficiently brown on top before it is cooked through, cover with a greased paper to prevent burning.

To test if done, dip a clean knife into hot water. Thrust it gently down the centre of cake. If done, the knife will come out clean and bright.

1. CAKE MIXTURE.

1/4 lb. butter, 1/4 lb. castor sugar, 6 ozs. flour, 2 eggs.

Half butter and half nutter gives just as good results and is more economical.

Beat together the butter and sugar to a cream. Whisk the eggs to a stiff froth and add. Stir in the flour gently. Mix well. Add a little milk if mixture is too stiff. This makes a Madeira Cake.

For other varieties, mix with the flour 1 dessertspoon caraway seeds for Seed Cake; 2 tablespoons desiccated cocoanut for Cocoanut Cake; 6 ozs. candied cherries chopped in halves for Cherry Cake; 6 ozs. sultanas and the grated rind of 1 lemon for Sultana Cake; the grated yellow part of 2 lemon rinds for Lemon Cake.

2. SMALL CAKES.

Take 2 small eggs and half quantities of the ingredients given for the cake mixture. Add the grated rind of half a lemon for flavouring. Grease a tin for small cakes with 9 depressions. Put a spoonful of the mixture in each depression. Bake for 20 minutes in a hot oven.

3. COCOANUT BISCUITS.

1/2 lb. desiccated cocoanut, 1/4 lb. sugar, 2 small eggs.

Proceed as for Macaroons, but make the cakes smaller. Bake in a moderate oven for half an hour.

4. "CORN WINE AND OIL" CAKES.

1 lb. wholemeal flour, 3/4 lb. raisins, 4 tablespoons walnut oil, 1/4 pint water.

This recipe was especially concocted for non-users of milk and eggs. Stir the oil well into the flour. Add the washed and stoned raisins (or seedless raisins, or sultanas). Mix to a dough with the water. Divide dough into two portions. Roll out, form into rounds, and cut each round into 6 small scones. Bake in a hot oven for half an hour.

5. CURRANT SANDWICH.

8 ozs. butter, 1 lb. flour, 1/4 lb. cane sugar, currants.

Mix flour and sugar, and rub in the butter. Mix with water to plastic dough. Divide dough into two cakes, 1 inch in thickness. Cover one evenly with currants, lay the other on top, and roll out to the thickness of one-third of an inch. Cut into sections, and bake in a hot oven for about 30 minutes.

6. APPLE SANDWICH.

Make a short crust (see recipe). Well grease some shallow jam sandwich tins. Roll out the paste very thin and line with it the tins. Peel, core, and finely chop some good, juicy apples. Spread well all over the paste. Sprinkle with castor sugar and grated lemon rind. Cover with another layer of thin paste. Bake for about 20 minutes in a hot oven. When done, take carefully out of the tin to cool. Cut into wedges, sprinkle with castor sugar, and pile on a plate.

7. FANCY BISCUITS.

8 ozs. flour, 4 ozs. butter, or 3 ozs. butter and 1 egg, 4 ozs. cane sugar, flavouring.

Flavouring may consist of lemon rind, desiccated cocoanut, cooked currants, carraway seed, mace, ginger, etc. Beat the butter and sugar to a cream, add flavouring and flour. Mix with the beaten egg, if used; it not, treat like the Lemon Short Cake. Roll out, cut into shapes, and bake about 10 minutes.

8. GINGER NUTS.

1/2 lb. nutter, 1/2 lb. sugar, 1 pint molasses or golden syrup, 1/2 oz. ground cloves and all-spice mixed, 2 tablespoons cinnamon, flour to form dough.

Beat the nutter and sugar together; add the molasses, spice, etc., and just enough flour to form a plastic dough. Knead well, roll out, cut into small biscuits, and bake on oiled or floured tins in a very moderate oven.

9. JAM SANDWICH.

Mix ingredients and prepare 2 jam sandwich tins as for Sponge Cake (see recipe). Pour mixture in tins and bake for about 10 minutes in a hot oven. Take out, spread one round with warmed jam, place the other on top, and cut when cold.

10. LEMON SHORT CAKE.

1 lb. flour, 7 ozs. nutter, 1/4 lb. sugar, rind of 1 lemon.

Mix together nutter and sugar, add grated lemon rind, work in flour, and knead well. Press into sheets about 1/2 in. thick. Prick all over. Bake in a moderate oven for about 20 minutes.

An easy way of baking for the inexpert cook who may find it difficult to avoid breaking the sheets, is to well grease a shallow jam-sandwich tin, sprinkle it well with castor sugar, as for sponge cakes, and press the short cake into it, well smoothing the top with a knife, and, lastly, pricking it.

II. MACAROONS. 5 ozs. sweet almonds, 5 ozs. castor sugar, 2 eggs.

Blanch the almonds and flake them in a nut mill. Whisk the eggs to a stiff froth adding the sugar a teaspoonful at a time. Add the almonds, and stir lightly. Drop the mixture, a dessertspoon at a time, on to well-oiled paper, or, better still, rice-paper. Shape with a knife into small cakes and put the half of a blanched almond into the centre of each. Bake in a moderate oven.

12. SPONGE CAKE.

Take the weight of two eggs in castor sugar and flour.

For a richer cake take the weight of two eggs in sugar and the weight of one only in flour.

Well grease the cake-tin, and sprinkle with castor sugar until thoroughly covered, and shake out any that remains loose.

Well whisk the eggs with a coiled wire beater. They must be quite stiff when done. Add the sugar, a teaspoon at a time, while whisking. Or separate the yolks and whites, beating the yolks and sugar together and whisking the whites on a plate with a knife before adding to the yolks. Lastly, dredge in the flour. Stir lightly, but do not beat, or the eggs will go down. Pour mixture into tin, and bake about one hour in a moderate oven.

13. SULTANA SCONES.

1 oz. cane sugar, 3 ozs. nutter, 1 lb. flour, 1/4 lb. sultanas, a short 1/2 pint water.

Mix the flour and sugar; rub in the nutter; add sultanas; make it into a dough with the water; roll out about 1/2 in. thick; form into scones; bake in a moderate oven.

14. SUSSEX CAKE.

1 lb. flour, 6 ozs. nutter, 1/4 lb. sultanas, 1/4 lb. castor sugar, grated lemon rind.

This cake is included especially for the non-users of milk and eggs. Of course it does not turn out quite like the orthodox cake; some people might even call it "puddeny," but it is not by any means unlike the substantial household cake if the directions are minutely followed and the baking well done. But if any attempt is made to make it rich, disaster follows, and it becomes as heavy as the proverbial lead. Made as follows, however, I am told it is quite common in some country places:—Beat the nutter and sugar to a cream. Upon the amount of air incorporated during this beating depends the lightness of the cake. Beat the flour into the creamed nutter. Now add enough water to make cake of a consistency to not quite drop off the spoon. Put the mixture into a greased hot qr. qtn. tin. Put in a very hot oven until nicely brown. This will take from 20 minutes to half an hour. Cover top with greased paper, and allow oven to get slightly cooler. The baking will take from 1-1/2 to 2 hours.

XI.—JAM, MARMALADE, &c.

Jam simply consists of fresh fruit boiled with a half to two-thirds its weight of white cane sugar until the mixture jellies.

Nearly every housekeeper has her own recipe for jam. One that I know of uses a whole pound of sugar to a pound of fruit and boils it for nearly two hours. The result is a very stiff, sweet jam, much more like shop jam than home-made jam. Its only recommendation is that it will keep for an unlimited time. Some recipes include water. But unless distilled water can be procured, it is better not to dilute the fruit. The only advantage gained is an increase of bulk. The jam may be made just as liquid by using rather less sugar in proportion to the fruit. A delicious jam is made by allowing 1/2 lb. sugar to every pound of fruit and cooking for half an hour from the time it first begins to boil. But unless this is poured immediately into clean, hot, dry jars, and tied down very tightly with parchment covers, it will not keep. Nevertheless, too much sugar spoils the flavour of the fruit, and too long boiling spoils the quality of the sugar. A copper or thick enamelled iron pan is needed.

The best recipe for ordinary use allows 3/4 lb. sugar to each pound fruit. Put the fruit in the pan with a little of the sugar, and when this boils, add the rest. Boil rather quickly for an hour. Keep well skimmed. Pour into hot, dry jars, and cover.

1. FRUIT NUT FILLING.

For small, open tarts, the following mixture is a good substitute for the lemon curd that goes to make cheese cakes. Peel, core and quarter some juicy apples. Put in a double saucepan (or covered jar) with some strips of lemon peel (yellow part only) and cane sugar to taste. Cook slowly to a pulp and, when cold, remove the lemon rind. Grate finely, or mill some Brazil nuts. Mix apple pulp and ground nut together in such proportions as to make a mixture of the consistency of stiff jam. Fill tarts with mixture and sprinkle top with ground nut. It must be used the same day as made.

2. JAM WITHOUT SUGAR.

To every pound of fresh fruit allow 1/2 lb. dates. Wash the fruit, put it in the preserving pan, and heat slowly, stirring well to draw out the juice. Wash and stone the dates. Add to the fruit, and simmer very gently for 45 minutes. Put immediately into clean, hot, dry jars, and tie on parchment covers at once.

3. LEMON CURD.

1 lb. lump sugar, 3 lemons (the rinds of 2 grated), yolks of 6 eggs, 1/4 lb. butter.

Put the butter into a clean saucepan; melt, but do not let it boil. Add the sugar, and stir until it is dissolved. Then add the beaten yolks, and, lastly, the grated lemon rind and juice. Stir over a slow fire until the mixture looks like honey and becomes thick. Put into jars, cover, and tie down as for jam.

4. MARMALADE.

To 1 large Seville orange (if small, count 3 as 2) allow 3/4 lb. cane sugar and 3/4 pint water. Wash and brush oranges, remove pips, cut peel into fine shreds (better still, put through a mincer). Put all to soak in the water for 24 hours. Boil until rinds are soft. Stand another 24 hours. Add the sugar, and boil until marmalade jellies. If preferred, half sweet and half Seville oranges may be used.

5. VEGETABLE MARROW JAM.

Peel the marrow, remove seeds, and cut into dice. To each pound of marrow allow 1 lb. cane sugar; to every 3 lbs. of marrow allow the juice and grated yellow part of rind of 1 lemon and 1/2 a level teaspoon ground ginger. Put the marrow into the preserving pan, sprinkle well with some of the sugar, and stand for 12 hours. Add the rest of the sugar, and boil slowly for 2 hours. Add the lemon juice, rind, and ginger at the end of 1-1/2 hours.

XII.—SALADS, BEVERAGES, &c.

1. SALAD.

Lettuce, tomatoes, mustard and cress, cucumber, olive or walnut oil, lemon juice.

Wash the green stuff and finely shred it. Peel the cucumber, skin the tomatoes (if ripe, the skins will come away easily) and cut into thin slices. Place in the bowl in alternate layers. Let the top layer be lettuce with a few slices of tomato for garnishing. Slices of hard-boiled egg may be added if desired.

For the salad dressing, to every tablespoonful of oil allow 1 of lemon juice. Drip the oil slowly into the lemon juice, beating with a fork all the time. Pour over the salad.

2. SALAD.

Beetroot, mustard and cress, olive or walnut oil, lemon juice, cold vegetables.

Chop the cold vegetables. French beans and potatoes make the nicest salad. To every 2 cups of vegetables allow 1 cup of chopped beetroot. Mix well together, and pour over salad dressing as for No. 1. A level teaspoonful of pepper is added to a gill of the dressing by those who do not object to its use.

3. FRUIT SALAD.

Take sweet, ripe oranges, apples, bananas, and grapes. Peel the oranges, quarter them, and remove skin and pips. Peel and core the apples and cut into thin slices. Wash and dry the grapes, and remove from stalks. Skin and slice the bananas.

Put the prepared fruit into a glass dish in alternate layers. Squeeze the juice from 2 sweet oranges and pour over the salad.

Any other fresh fruit in season may be used for this salad. Castor sugar may be sprinkled over if desired, and cream used in place of the juice. Grated nuts are also a welcome addition.

4. LEMON CORDIAL.

12 lemons, 1 lb. lump sugar.

Put the sugar into a clean saucepan. Grate off the yellow part of the rinds of 6 lemons and sprinkle over the sugar. Now moisten the sugar with as much water as it will absorb. Boil gently to a clear syrup. Add the juice from the lemons, stir well, and pour into clean, hot, dry bottles. Cork tightly and cover with sealing-wax or a little plaster-of-Paris mixed with water and laid on quickly. Add any quantity preferred to cold or hot water to prepare beverage, or use neat as sauce for puddings.

5. LIME CORDIAL. The same as for Lemon, but use 13 limes.

6. ORANGE CORDIAL.

The same as for Lemon, but use 3/4 lb. sugar.

A detailed list of Fruit and Herb Teas will be found in the companion volume to this, "Food Remedies."

7. WALLACE CHEESE.

1 qt. milk, 6 tablespoons lemon juice.

Strain the lemon juice and pour it into the boiling milk. Lay a piece of fine, well-scalded muslin over a colander. Pour the curdled milk into this. When it has drained draw the edges of the muslin together and squeeze and press the cheese. Leave it in the muslin in the colander, with a weight on it for 12 hours. It will then be ready to serve.

This cheese is almost tasteless, and many people prefer it so. But if the flavour of lemon is liked, use more lemon juice. The whey squeezed from the cheese is a wholesome drink when quite fresh.

XIII.—EXTRA RECIPES.

1. BARLEY WATER.

1 dessert spoon Robinson's "Patent" Barley, 1/2 a lemon, 3 lumps cane sugar.

Rub the lumps of sugar on the lemon until they are bright yellow in colour and quite wet. (It is the fragrant juice contained in the yellow surface of the lemon rind that gives the delicious lemon flavour without acidity.) Mix the barley to a thin paste with a little cold water. This is poured into a pint of boiling water, well stirred until it comes to the boil again and then left to boil for five minutes, after which it is done. Add the sugar and lemon juice.

2. BOILED HOMINY.

Take one part of Hominy and 2-1/2 parts of water. Have the water boiling; add the hominy and boil for fifteen minutes; keep stirring to keep from burning.

3. BROWN GRAVY.

1 dessert-spoon butter, 1 dessert-spoon white flour, hot water.

Melt the butter in a small iron saucepan or frying pan and sprinkle into it the flour. Keep stirring gently with a wooden spoon until the flour is a rich dark brown, but not burnt, or the flavour will be spoilt. Then add very gently, stirring well all the time, rather less than half-a-pint of hot water. Stir until the mixture boils, when it should be a smooth brown gravy to which any flavouring may be added. Strained tomato pulp is a nice addition, but a teaspoonful of lemon juice will suffice.

4. BUTTERED RICE AND PEAS.

1 cup unpolished rice, 3 cups water, 2 cups fresh-shelled peas, 1 tablespoon finely chopped parsley, 1 teaspoon lemon juice, butter size of walnut.

Put the rice on in the water and bring gradually to the boil. Boil hard for five minutes, stirring once or twice. Draw it to side of stove, where it is comparatively cool, or, if a gas stove is used, put the saucepan on an asbestos mat and turn the gas as low as possible. The water should now gradually steam away, leaving the rice dry and well cooked.

Steam the peas in a separate pan. If young, about 20 minutes should be sufficient; they are spoiled by over-cooking.

Add the cooked peas to the cooked rice, with the butter, parsley, and lemon juice. Stir over the fire until the mixture is thoroughly hot.

Serve with or without tomato sauce and new potatoes.

5. CONVALESCENTS' SOUP.

1 small head celery, 1 large onion, 1 carrot, 1 turnip, 3 tablespoons coarsely chopped parsley, P.R. Barley malt meal, Mapleton's or P.R. almond or pine-

kernel cream, 3 pints boiling water.

Well wash the vegetables and slice them, and add them with the parsley to the boiling water. (The water should be distilled, if possible, and the cooking done in a large earthenware jar or casserole. See notes *re* casseroles in Chap. IV.) Simmer gently for 2 hours, or until quite soft. Then strain through a hair sieve. Do not rub the vegetables through the sieve to make a purée, simply strain and press all the juices out. The vegetable juices are all wanted, but not the fibre. To each pint of this vegetable broth allow 1 heaped tablespoon barley malt meal, 1 tablespoon nut cream, and 1/2 lb. tomatoes. Mix the meal to a thin paste with some of the cooled broth (from the pint). Put the rest of the pint in a saucepan or casserole and bring to the boil. Add the meal and boil for 10 minutes. Break up the tomatoes and cook slowly to a pulp (without water). Rub through a sieve. (The skin and pips are not to be forced through.) Add this pulp to the soup. Lastly mix the nut-cream to a thin cream by dripping slowly a little water or cool broth into it, stirring hard with a teaspoon all the time. Add this to the soup, re-heat, but do *not* boil, serve.

This soup is rather irksome to make, but is intensely nourishing and easy of digestion. The pine-kernel cream is the more digestible of the two creams. Care should be taken not to *cook* these nut creams. If the soup is for an invalid care should also be taken that, while getting all the valuable vegetable juices, no skin or pips, etc., are included. The vegetable broth may be prepared a day in advance, but it will not keep for three days except in very cold weather. (When it is desired to keep soup it should be brought to the boil with the lid of the stockpot or casserole on, and put away without the lid being removed or the contents stirred.)

6. FINE OATMEAL BISCUITS.

2 ozs. flour, 3-1/2 ozs. Robinson's "Patent" Groats, 2 ozs. castor sugar, 2 ozs. butter, 2 eggs.

Cream the butter and sugar, add the eggs, then the flour and groats, which should be mixed together. Roll out thin and cut out with a cutter. Bake in a moderate oven until a light colour.

7. FINE OATMEAL GRUEL.

1 heaped tablespoon Robinson's "Patent" Groats, 1 pint milk or water.

Mix the groats with a wineglassful of cold water, gradually added, into a smooth paste, pour this into a stew-pan containing nearly a pint of boiling water or milk, stir the gruel on the fire (while it boils) for ten minutes.

8. MACARONI CHEESE.

1/4 lb. macaroni, 1-1/2 ozs. cheese, 1/2 pint milk, 1 teaspoon flour, butter, pepper.

The curled macaroni is the best among the ordinary kinds. Better still, however, is the macaroni made with fine wholemeal flour which is stocked by some food-reform stores. Parmesan cheese is nicest for this dish. Stale cheese spoils it.

Wash the macaroni. Put it into fast-boiling water and keep boiling until *very* tender. Drain off the water and replace it with the 1/2 pint of milk. Bring to the boil and stir in the flour mixed to a thin paste with cold milk or water. Simmer for 5 minutes. Grate the cheese finely.

Butter a shallow pie-dish. Put the thickened milk and macaroni in alternate layers with the grated cheese. Dust each layer with pepper, if liked. Top with grated cheese. Put some small pieces of butter on top of the grated cheese. Put in a very hot oven until nicely browned.

9. MANHU HEALTH CAKE.

1/4 lb. butter, 1/2 lb. castor sugar, 1/2 lb. Manhu flour, 1 oz. rice flour, 6 ozs. crystallised ginger, 4 eggs.

Cream butter and sugar, adding eggs, two at once, not beaten. Beat each time after adding eggs, add rice flour, ginger, and lastly flour. Bake in moderate oven.

10. MANHU HOMINY PUDDING.

1-1/2 teacupfuls of boiled Hominy (see below), 1 pint or less of sweet milk, 1/2 teacupful of sugar, 2 eggs (well beaten), 1 teacupful of raisins, spice to taste.

Mix together and bake twenty minutes in a moderately hot oven. Serve hot with cream and sugar or sauce.

11. PARKIN.

2 ozs. butter, 2 ozs. moist sugar, 6 ozs. best treacle, 1/2 lb. medium oatmeal, 1/4 lb. flour, 1/2 oz. powdered ginger, grated rind of 1 lemon.

Some people prefer the addition of carraway seeds to lemon rind. If these are used a level teaspoonful will be sufficient for the quantities given above. The old-fashioned black treacle is almost obsolete now, and is replaced commercially by golden syrup, many brands of which are very pale and of little flavour. To make successful Parkin a good brand of pure cane syrup is needed. I always use "Glebe." This is generally only stocked by a few "high-class " grocers or large stores, but it is worth the trouble of getting. Some Food Reform Stores stock molasses, and this was probably used for the original Parkin. It is strongly flavoured and blacker than black treacle, but its taste is not unpleasant. For the sugar, a good brown moist cane sugar, like Barbados, is best. Put the treacle and butter (or nutter) into a jar and put into a warm oven until the butter is dissolved. Then stir in the sugar. Mix together the oatmeal, flour, ginger and seeds or lemon rind. Pour the treacle, etc., into this, and mix to a paste. Roll out lightly on a well-floured board to a 1/4 inch thickness. Bake in a well-greased flat tin for about 50 minutes, in a rather slow oven. To test if done, dip a skewer into boiling water, wipe, and thrust into the Parkin; if it comes out clean the latter is done. Cut into squares, take out of tin, and allow to cool.

12. PROTOSE CUTLETS.

1 lb. minced Protose, 1 lb. plain boiled rice, 1 small grated onion, 1/2 teaspoon sage.

Mix the ingredients with a little milk; shape into cutlets, using uncooked macaroni for the bone, and bake in a moderate oven about 45 minutes.

13. PROTOSE SALAD.

1 breakfast-cupful Protose cubes, 1/3 breakfast cup minced celery, 1 hard-boiled egg, 3 small radishes, juice of 2 lemons.

Cut Protose into cubes, chop the hard-boiled egg, slice the radishes. Add to the minced celery. Pour over these ingredients the lemon juice and allow the mixture to stand for one hour. Serve upon fresh crisp lettuce.

14. RISOTTO.

3/4 lb. rice, 1/2 lb. cheese, 4 large onions.

Slice and fry the onions in a stew-pan in a little fat; when brown, add 1-1/2 pints water and the rice. Let it cook about an hour, and then add the grated cheese.

This dish may be varied with tomatoes when in season.

15. ROYAL NUT ROAST.

1/2 lb. pine kernels, 2 medium-sized tomatoes, 1 medium onion, 2 new-laid eggs.

Wash, dry and pick over the pine kernels and put them through the macerating machine. Skin and well mash the tomatoes. Grate finely the onion. Mix all together and beat to a smooth batter. Whisk the eggs to a stiff froth and add to the mixture. Pour into a greased pie-dish. Bake in a moderate oven until a golden-brown colour. It should "rise" like a cake. It may be eaten warm with brown gravy or tomato sauce, or cold with salad.

16. STEWED NUTTOLENE.

Slice one half-pound nuttolene into a baking dish, adding water enough to cover nicely. Place it in the oven, and let it bake for an hour. A piece of celery may be added to give flavour, or a little mint. When done, thicken the water with a little flour, and serve.

17. WELSH RAREBIT.

Cheese, butter, bread, pepper.

Cut thin slices of cheese and put them with a little butter into a saucepan. When well melted pour over hot well-buttered toast. Dust with pepper. Put into a very hot oven for a few minutes and serve.

18. YEAST BREAD.

7 lbs. flour, salt to taste (about 3/4 ounce), 1 ounce yeast, 1-1/2 quarts of warm water.

Put the flour into a pan or large basin, add salt to taste, and mix it well in. Put the yeast with a lump of sugar into a small basin, and pour a little of the *warm* water on to if. Cold or hot water kills the yeast. Leave this a little while until the yeast bubbles, then smooth out all lumps and pour into a hole made in the middle of the flour. Pour in the rest of the warm water, and begin to stir in the flour. Now begin kneading the dough, and knead until the whole is smooth and damp, and leaves the hand without sticking, which will take about 15 to 20 minutes. Time spent in kneading is not wasted.

Set the pan in a warm place, covered with a clean cloth. Be careful not to put the pan where it can get too hot. The fender is a good place, but to the side of the fire rather than in front. Let it rise at least an hour, but should it not have risen very much—say double the size—let it stand longer, as the bread cannot be light if the dough has not risen sufficiently.

Now have a baking-board well floured, and turn all the dough on to it. Have tins or earthenware pans, or even pie-dishes well greased. Divide the dough, putting enough to half fill the pans or tins. Put these on the fender to rise again for 20 to 30 minutes, then bake in a hot oven, about 350 degrees (a little hotter than for pastry).

Bake (for a loaf about 2 lbs. in a moderate oven) from 30 to 40 minutes. Of course the time depends greatly on the size of the loaves and the heat of the oven.

The above recipe produces the ordinary white loaf. Better bread would, in my opinion, result from the use of a very fine wholemeal flour such as the "Nu-Era," and the omission of salt.

XV.—WEIGHTS AND MEASURES AND UTENSILS.

If possible sieve all flour before measuring, as maggots are *sometimes* to be found therein; also because tightly-compressed flour naturally measures less than flour which has been well shaken up.

1 lb. = 16 ozs. = 3 teacupsful or 2 breakfastcupsful, closely filled, but not heaped.

1/2 lb. = 8 ozs. = 1 breakfastcupful, closely filled, but not heaped.

1/4 lb. = 4 ozs. = 1 teacupful, loosely filled.

1 oz. = 2 tablespoonsful, filled level.

1/2 oz. = 1 tablespoonful, filled level.

1/4 oz. = 1 dessertspoonful, filled level.

4 gills = 1 pint = 3-1/2 teacupsful, or nearly 2 breakfastcupsful.

1 gill = 1 small teacupful.

10 unbroken eggs weigh about 1 lb.

1 oz. butter = 1 tablespoon heaped as much above the spoon as the spoon rounds underneath.

USEFUL UTENSILS.

BAKING DISHES.—Earthenware are the best.

BREAD GRATER.—The simple tin grater, price 1d., grates bread, vegetables, lemon rind, etc.

BASINS.—Large for mixing, small for puddings, etc.

EGG SLICE.—For dishing up rissoles, etc.

EGG WHISK.—The coiled wire whisk, price 1d. or 2d., is the best.

FOOD CHOPPER.—See that it has the nut-butter attachment.

FRYING BASKET and stew-pan to fit.

FRYING AND OMELET PANS.—Cast aluminium are the best.

GEM PANS.

JARS.—Earthenware jars for stewing.

JUGS.—Wide-mouthed jugs are easiest to clean.

JELLY AND BLANC MANGE MOULDS.

LEMON SQUEEZER.—The glass squeezer is the best.

MARMALADE CUTTER.

NUT MILL.

NUTMEG GRATER.

PALETTE KNIFE.—For beating white of egg, scraping basins, etc.

PASTE BOARD and ROLLING PIN.

PESTLE and MORTAR.

PRESERVING PAN.—Copper or enamelled.

RAISIN SEEDER.

SAUCEPANS.—Cast aluminium are the best.

SCALES AND WEIGHTS.

SIEVES.—Hair and wire.

STILL.—For distilling water.

STRAINERS.

TINS.—Cake tin, qr. qtn. tin, vegetable and pastry cutters.

XVI.—MENUS.

The menus given below do not follow the conventional lines which ordain that a menu shall include, at least, soup, savoury and sweet dishes. The hardworking housewife can afford neither the time nor the material to serve up so many dishes at one meal; and the wise woman does not desire to spend any more time and material on the needs of the body than will suffice to keep it strong and healthy. Lack of space will not allow me to include many menus. I have only attempted to give the barest suggestions for two weeks. But a study of the rest of the book will enable anyone to extend and elaborate them. Three meals a day are the most that are necessary, and no woman desires to cook more than once a day. If possible the cooked meal should be the mid-day one. Late dinners may be fashionable, but they are not wholesome. If the exigencies of work make the evening meal the principal one, let it be taken as early as possible.

WARMING UP.

It often happens that while the father of a family needs his dinner when he comes home in the evening, it is necessary to provide a mid-day dinner for the others, especially if children are included. Many housewives thus go to the labour of preparing a hot dinner twice a day, but this may be avoided if the following directions are carefully carried out:—Prepare the mid-day meal as if the father were at home, and serve him first. Put his portion—savoury, vegetables and gravy—in one soup plate, and cover it immediately with another. Do the same with the pudding, and put both dishes away in the pantry. A good hour before they are wanted put into a warm oven. (If a gas oven is used, see that there is plenty of hot water in the floor pan.)

When quite hot the food should not be in the least dried up. This is ensured by having the oven warm, but not hot, warming up the food slowly, and, in the first place, covering closely with the soup plate while still hot, so that the steam does not escape. I have eaten many dinners saved for me in this way, and should never have known they were not just cooked if I had not been told. Of course, a boiled plain pudding or plum pudding can be returned to its basin and steamed and extra gravy saved and reheated in the tureen.

SUNDAY AND MONDAY.

The cook needs a day of rest once a week as well as other people. And this should be on a Sunday if possible, so that she may participate in the recreations of the other members of her family. This is more easily attainable in summer than in winter, for in hot weather many persons prefer a cold dinner. But even in winter, soups, vegetable stews, nut roasts, baked fruit pies, and boiled puddings can all be made the day before. They will all reheat without spoiling in the least.

Monday is the washing-day in many households, and no housewife wants to cook on that day. In flesh-eating households cold meat forms the staple article of diet. The vegetarian housewife cannot do better than prepare a large plain pudding on the Saturday, boil it for two hours, put it away in its basin, and boil it two hours again on Monday; with what is left over from Sunday, this will probably be sufficient for Monday's dinner.

BREAKFASTS.

A sufficient breakfast may consist simply of bread and nut butter, with the addition of an apple or other fresh fruit. A good substitute for tea and coffee is a fruit soup. Where porridge and milk are taken, this would probably not be needed. Eggs, cooked tomatoes, marmalade, and grated nuts are all welcome additions.

HIGH TEAS.

If tea is taken, let it be as weak as possible. Do not let it stand for more than three minutes after making, but pour it immediately off from the leaves into another pot. See that the latter is hot.

Some of the simpler savoury dishes (omelets, etc.) may be taken at this meal if desired. Also lentil and nut pastes, salads, Wallace cheese, raisin bread, oatcake, sweet cakes and biscuits, jams, etc.

DINNERS.

SUNDAY.—Hot nut roast and brown gravy; steamed potatoes and cabbage; fruit tart and custard.

MONDAY.—Cold nut roast and salad; bubble and squeak; plain pudding and golden syrup.

TUESDAY.—Haricot rissoles and tomato sauce; baked potatoes; milk pudding and stewed fruit, or apple and tapioca pudding.

WEDNESDAY.—Lentil soup; jam roll.

THURSDAY.—Lentil soup; fig pudding.

FRIDAY.—Hot pot; roasted pine kernels; steamed potatoes and cauliflowers; railway pudding.

SATURDAY. Irish stew; boiled rice and stewed prunes.

SUNDAY. Vegetable stew; batter pudding; steamed potatoes and cauliflower; summer pudding.

MONDAY. Stewed lentils; baked tomatoes or onions, and sauté potatoes; milk pudding and stewed fruit.

TUESDAY.—Stewed celery or other vegetable in season; roasted pine kernels; mashed potatoes; apple dumplings.

WEDNESDAY.—Barley broth; treacle pudding.

THURSDAY.—Barley broth; Bombay pudding.

FRIDAY.—Macaroni and tomatoes; chip potatoes; nut pastry.

SATURDAY.—Toad-in-the-hole; baked potatoes; jam tart.

NOTE. The same soup is indicated on two consecutive days in order to save labour. Few persons object to the same dish twice if it is not to be repeated again for some time. And unless the family be very large, it is as easy to make enough soup for two days as for one.

www.ingramcontent.com/pod-product-compliance
Lightning Source LLC
Chambersburg PA
CBHW081627100526
44590CB00021B/3628